This Book Is
Protected by
Instant IP

REFERABLE

How to Get Unlimited Introductions Without Even Asking

REFERABLE

How to Get Unlimited Introductions Without Even Asking

David Van Buskirk

Printed in the United States of America

Published by Igniting Souls
PO Box 43, Powell, OH 43065
IgnitingSouls.com

LCCN: 2025927457

Paperback ISBN: 978-1-63680-600-6
Hardback ISBN: 978-1-63680-601-3
eBook ISBN: 978-1-63680-602-0

Available in paperback, hardcover, e-book, and audiobook.

Any Internet addresses (websites, blogs, etc.) and telephone numbers printed in this book are offered as a resource. They are not intended in any way to be or imply an endorsement by Igniting Souls, nor does Igniting Souls vouch for the content of these sites and numbers for the life of this book.

Some names and identifying details may have been changed to protect the privacy of individuals.

The content of this book reflects the author's personal experiences, opinions, and interpretations. The inclusion of any individual, living or deceased, or any organization or entity, is not intended to malign, defame, or harm the reputation of such persons or entities. All statements regarding individuals are solely the author's perspective and do not represent verified facts unless expressly cited to a verifiable source.

The publisher has not independently investigated or confirmed the accuracy of any such references and disclaims all responsibility for them. Nothing in this book should be construed as factual assertions about the character, conduct, or reputation of any individual or entity mentioned. Any resemblance to persons living or dead is purely coincidental unless explicitly stated.

The publisher expressly disclaims liability for any alleged loss, damage, or injury arising from any perceived defamatory content or reliance upon statements within this work. Responsibility for the views, depictions, and representations rests solely with the author.

The superscript symbol IP listed throughout this book is known as the unique certification mark created and owned by Instant IP[IP]. Its use signifies that the corresponding expression (words, phrases, chart, graph, etc.) has been protected by Instant IP[IP] via smart contract. Instant IP[IP] is designed with the patented smart contract solution (US Patent: 11,928,748), which creates an immutable time-stamped first layer and fast layer identifying the moment in time an idea is filed on the blockchain. This solution can be used in defending intellectual property protection. Infringing upon the respective intellectual property, i.e., IP, is subject to and punishable in a court of law.

Table of Contents

PART THREE: PRODIGIOUS

Preface

THIS BOOK IS short for a reason. Entrepreneurs and sales professionals are busier than ever. Every day brings a new flood of information. If you're like me, you love reading business books, but they take too much time to get through. Books are long when they are filled with stories, and while these stories can add value, authors often include them in an attempt to bring more attention to themselves rather than keeping the focus on the reader.

The principles presented in this book are meant to help you become more referable. When you turn the next few pages, you won't have to read story after story about how someone else has become more referable. Instead, you will find truths and practical principles that hopefully remind you of stories from your own business or businesses you have worked with. So, as you read, consider your experiences and how the principles relate to you.

Because this book is brief, enjoy it during a short flight, read for a few minutes each night before you go to sleep, listen to it while you take a walk, or pick it up during some weekend downtime. However you see fit to enjoy it, I hope you walk away feeling seen and referable.

Thank you for your interest in this little book.

Predictable

Do You Really Want to Settle for Average?

DURING THE FIRST week of every calendar year, our office notices an uptick in phone calls. Each one of those first few business days brings us a few new referrals. Why then? Because people gather with their families during those last two weeks of December, and we've discovered they talk about us!

It's not that we don't ask our clients to send their friends. Of course, we do. When you help people, and they feel like you care about them, it comes up in conversation.

From a very young age, my mother and father instilled in their children the idea of always doing the right thing. The golden rule—do unto others as you would have them do unto you—was a big part of my and my sister's upbringing. But what young child imagines that their parents' advice will become the key to a successful business?

Think about the last time you dealt with another professional. What was your experience? Did they leave a wonderfully positive impression? Will you use their services again? What drives that decision?

More than a few businesspeople deal with today leave them slightly underwhelmed. It's not that the business did anything wrong. But there wasn't anything tremendously magnetic about the experience either. These underwhelming companies will continue to do business for years. Sadly, their customer turnover will be tremendous, and they'll never know most of their clients' names. Marketing takes up a huge chunk of the budget for most of these businesses, and once or twice a year, they'll hear a new customer mention someone who referred them, but the business owner usually doesn't have a clue who the referral came from.

You can keep running your business in the mode of mediocrity, but it's hard work.

Word of Mouth

Regardless of how businesses report the numbers, nearly every source will tell you that word-of-mouth advertising always proves most effective. If that's the case, and we all know we would like to receive more referrals, how do you get them?

Strategic Coach® is a tremendous coaching program I've been a part of for almost two decades. I'm forever grateful for my brother from another mother, Jeff Cardella, for introducing me to the program and for the friendship we have built since. Co-founder Dan Sullivan says entrepreneurs ask the wrong question. "Instead of 'What's the best way to ask for referrals?'" Dan says," You should ask, 'Am I running a referable business?'"

We're more likely to trust the experience of our friends and family than any web search or social media ad. And we give their stories of poor service as much credence as we do the ones of good service.

As a business leader, it's essential to recognize what kind of impression we leave our clients with. When they tell the people closest to them about the time they spent with you, will it sound like an ordeal or a pleasant experience?

Be Kind

I was blessed to be raised by tremendous parents and grandparents. Their lessons influenced the principles you'll find in this book. One of the last things my dad ever said to me encompasses the philosophy behind the Referable Framework.

In December of 2020, my dad had a heart attack—the widow maker that so few survive. Everyone in the family immediately flew to New Jersey to be with him. Due to the COVID pandemic, hospitals didn't allow visitors, not even from loved ones. Only my mother could go in. So, after he was stable in the ICU and things looked promising, we returned to Texas.

After five weeks in intensive care, doctors called my mom to say his heart couldn't be mended, and they let my sisters and their spouses, my niece, and my nephew in with my mom to visit since he wouldn't be around much longer.

As soon as we got the call, we got tickets and headed for the airport. And as we boarded the plane, we made a FaceTime call to my father. He was more alert than he had been in any FaceTime call for the past five weeks, and he told us he was ready to go. Poppy, as the grandkids called him, told us, "I'm very proud of you. I love you, and I want to leave you with this one thing: Keep being kind to people." We said our goodbyes just before we took off.

I feel incredibly grateful to have had that final conversation with him before we turned our phones off. The plane didn't land in New Jersey before he left us, so the last thing my dad ever told me was "Be kind." It was almost as if he needed to remind us before he left this world.

It seems like a simple principle; however, when we look around and consider the way people treat each other on a regular basis, we come to the conclusion that common courtesy isn't as common as it should be.

The Referability Framework

Even before my dad shared his last words, the way my office treats people was a high business priority. We like to say, "When people do business with us, it is unlike any other business that they do business with.[IP]" The reason the experience is so different for our clients really comes down to the golden rule, as I've mentioned. The beautiful thing about this rule is how it flows seamlessly from your personal life into your professional practice. I'm blessed because my parents and grandparents modeled the golden rule. And when I found the love of my life, I discovered hers did as well. Because of this, Julie and I raised our children to treat people well, too.

I am tremendously fortunate to work for a company that trains its advisors in practicing these principles of kindness from day one. For over twenty-five years, they have always emphasized putting clients first and promoted a spirit of volunteering and paying it forward. I feel grateful to work among so many phenomenal advisors and home office associates.

My amazing team members have been practicing the golden rule long before I ever met them, and they continue to better themselves every day. Kendra and Karen have been with me for the past eight years. Almost daily, clients tell me I have the best team they've ever worked with. I have been incredibly lucky to have all the branch team members I have had over my twenty-five years.

Sadly, when the average person experiences kindness and thoughtfulness in a business setting, it surprises them. None of the things I'm about to share falls into the category of trade secrets. Our firm simply strives to always be kind and demonstrate an attitude of gratitude. Yes, we do it with some flair and intentionality, but so few businesses put the simplest of these Eight Principles into practice that those who do seem extraordinary. By implementing the Eight Principles of the

Referable Framework[IP] into our processes, we've become dinner conversation:

1. Manners Invite You to Tables You Would Never See Otherwise
2. Talking Less Influences More
3. Your Interest in Others Makes You More Interesting
4. Clear Commitments and Follow Through Close the Trust Gap
5. Find Unique Ways to Reach Out to Let People Know You Care
6. Shortcuts Undermine the Long Game
7. Take Care of Your Team, and They Will Take Care of You
8. Communicate Compliments; Keep Complaints

Maybe you noticed none of the Eight Principles specifically mention being thankful or expressing gratitude. That's because these attributes belong in each of the principles. Gratitude is the foundation of servant leadership. My coach, Lee Brower, embodies the lifestyle of a servant leader. In fact, the entire staff at Strategic Coach exudes this mindset. I feel blessed to have become part of such an organization. Lee often talks about the importance of expressing thanks in every part of our lives. Gratitude is bigger than a single principle. It's the underpinning of a referable culture, the keystone of a life well lived. So, you'll find gratitude intertwined throughout the process.

Fortunately, anyone can incorporate the basics of being Referable into their daily life. That's the best part of these principles. They aren't limited to business. They have the power to make people notice you wherever you go. Whether you're in the grocery line, a patron at a restaurant, or trying to become a multi-million-dollar business, if you implement this list of timeless truths, you'll become unbelievably Referable.

PART TWO

Principles

Principle One

Manners Invite You to "Tables" You Would Never Otherwise See

THE EMAIL HAD only two words, "Call me." My first thought was, "Do I work for this guy?" The person wanted me to promote his product to my clients, but I had to wonder if he appreciated the time I spent listening to him. His simple directive sounded like an order.

Sadly, in a world of quick texts and social media responses, this kind of language has become normal, but that's why people who add a few simple words to their communication stand out.

Manners Give Your Business an Edge

My parents introduced me to and demonstrated the importance of this First Principle from the day I was born. They taught me the art of appreciation and respect at an early age. Maybe that's why Mister Rogers, the creator and star of the PBS children's show Mister Rogers' Neighborhood, is still, to this day, one of my heroes.

The way he treated people had a profound impact on me. I sensed that his manners contributed to his popularity. Even famous 1980s talk show hosts like David Letterman and Johnny Carson were won over by his deep respect and quiet mannerisms.

Words like 'please' and 'thank you' make you more attractive at work and in real-life situations. And they'll make your business more attractive too.

An Order Becomes a Request, a Referral Becomes an Opportunity

A simple 'please' in that salesman's language could have changed the tone of his message entirely. Instead of an order, the communication becomes the request he intended it to be. People won't always say "yes" just because you use manners, but they might say "no" because you didn't.

'Thank you' works the same way. I frequently offer referrals to my clients. People our office helps need lawyers and CPAs, things out of our areas of expertise. I find it astounding how many professionals don't follow up with a thank you after I send them a referral. And I have to wonder, if they don't show me a moment of gratitude for my efforts, how do they treat my clients?

We feel honored when someone recommends our office to their friends or clients, and our team shows our appreciation with a note or a phone call. Referrals put food on our tables, and we don't want to ever take that for granted.

Which attorney do you think I will refer the next time one of my clients has a legal matter they need to take care of—the one who said thank you or the one who didn't acknowledge my effort?

When Manners Become Part of the Process

As I mentioned, the digital world has stolen some of our manners; however, the speed of business hasn't helped either. If you're doing your job right, you're probably busy. It's easy to let those few simple steps fall through the cracks when you're hurrying off to the next appointment, or you hear the beep of another call coming through.

These three words make up Dan Sullivan's top referability trait. Dan says, "Please shows respect, and Thank You shows appreciation." Why would someone want to do business with you if you don't show respect and gratitude?

To ensure our office doesn't let busyness get in the way of good manners, we've intentionally incorporated them into our processes.

First, regardless of why someone calls, we must say thank you before hanging up. Some clients call for their account balance or to get help with paperwork. Our process says the call ends something like this:

Our staff starts with, "Can I help with anything else today?"

"I think we covered it."

"Great! Thank you so much for calling today."

"No, No," the client says, "Thank you for helping me!"

"We just want you to know how grateful we are that you chose us. Thank you for making me feel useful today."

I'll admit, there have been times when I've been busy and forgotten to end the call with a thank-you. When that happens, as soon as I realize it, I pick up the phone and call back. "I hope you don't mind me calling again. I forgot something very important when we were on the phone last time. I'm so sorry. I forgot to tell you how much we appreciate you. Thank you for choosing us today."

Little courtesies like this surprise the client. They tell us, "You didn't have to do that." And they're right. We didn't have to. We want to. We know how these little efforts make us feel, and everyone in our office wants to pass them along.

Common Courtesy

Being polite isn't just part of our process; it's embedded in our culture. Our entire team knows they have permission to call one another out if they hear a phone call end without a simple thank you. Yet, the person who forgot feels grateful that someone reminded them. We all want it to become a habit. We know how much appreciation changes the atmosphere of our office, and we want that positivity to extend to our clients.

Polite also means speaking in simple terms. It's easy to rattle off acronyms or statistics or overexplain our plans. We aim to keep the conversation on a level our clients can understand. When you want to know what time it is, you don't care how the clock works. And when you ask a mechanic to change your brakes, you don't need to know which tools he will use or what the underside of your car looks like. The same is true of our clients. They don't need to know how to build your product to trust you know what you're doing. Throwing out information they don't need might make you sound intelligent, but you'll build deeper trust when the person on the other side of the table doesn't leave wondering what you just said. Keeping it simple is just another sign of respect.

When manners become part of the everyday workings of your business, you'll see exponential impact. People who feel your respect and appreciation assume you will show that same care to their friends and family. Manners have become so scarce in our society that those who show respect stand out, and those who feel that respect become your number one salespeople.

Implementation

Implementing courtesies in your business will make you stand out. And if you practice Principle One with your children, amazing things happen.

After Julie and I had children, we made sure they saw Mister Rogers' reruns or watched clips on YouTube®. Sarah, Ben, and Rachel all learned to enjoy the Neighborhood as much as I did. During our youngest's high school years, she often asked if we could watch Mr. Rogers together, and when the documentary came out in 2019, the family took me to see it for Father's Day.

Over the last two decades, we've often been complimented on our kids' behavior and how much they stand out because they're responsible. People can count on them, and they often demonstrate how much they care about their friends and family. But even more, they show respect with their manners.

To see if you're Referable, consider how well you implement Principle One in your life or business.

- How often did you use "please" and "thank you" last week?
- Do you show appreciation whenever you have an opportunity?
- We add 'thank you' to the end of every phone call, but where could you intentionally add these words so more people feel respect and gratitude?
- If you have children, pay attention to their actions. Kids are known to reflect our manners.

Principle Two

Talking Less
Influences More

MY DAD'S MOTHER loved spending one-on-one time with each of her eleven grandchildren. And she treated each of us as if we were the most important person in the world. Anytime she had an opportunity to be with me, we sat together at the kitchen table, and she started asking questions. Then she did something remarkable; she listened. My grandmother only spoke enough to encourage us to start talking again. The time she devoted to me made me feel significant and loved. I knew I could trust her with my secrets.

This element of trust is sorely missing from most businesses today. Stop and think about the people you interact with. How many of them do you trust completely? Which ones do you hope you can trust, and which do you stay guarded about?

From the moment our office starts interacting with a potential client, we work to move them into this zone of trust. We call the space between the introductory phone call and gaining their confidence the "Trust Gap[IP]". Referable businesses close the Trust Gap as quickly as possible.

Open-Ended Questions Close the Trust Gap

My grandmother's practice made all her grandchildren feel like she cared about us, and our team tries our best to implement this in our phone calls and annual reviews. In every conversation, we want to know what's most important to the client. We ask about what's happening with their family and what we can help with. We might even ask what's keeping them up at night.

Grandma taught me the importance of asking great questions and then shutting up and listening. She introduced me to Principle Two: Talking Less Influences More. Every coach I've worked with throughout my career has given me words of wisdom to build on this principle. Lee Brower, Dan Sullivan, Kim Butler, and the rest of the marvelous leadership at Strategic Coach; Don Connelly; Tom Bartow and Jason Selk of Selk-Bartow Coaching; John Bowen at CEG Worldwide®; sales coach Ari Galper; and especially my early and ongoing training from the firm I'm with all expand this concept for me.

Ari shares a philosophy that encourages an informal "get-to-know-you" meeting before the first meeting. One of the first times I used this strategy, I met with a recently divorced single mom who had been referred to us. During that first twenty-minute introduction meeting, I asked about her financial concerns and her background. I asked no more than five questions and offered no advice or information about our practice or the way we do business. I just let her talk.

When we finished, I set up our first meeting so we could go into her situation more in depth. That's when I would go through our discovery process with our full list of questions.

Within half an hour, the client who introduced us called. "Oh my gosh, Dave. Ann loves you. She said you were amazing."

"Really? I barely said anything," I told him.

Evidently, because I slowed down and listened, she thought I was the greatest guy in the world. I realized more than ever before that the one who talks least wins.

John Bowen, founder of CEG Worldwide, runs a coaching program for financial advisors. Though we didn't meet until we were adults, both of us were born in Owego, New York, and his parents and mine were great friends. But more importantly, his skills helped me enhance my use of open-ended questions. The things I learned from my time with his program helped us develop the questions we ask at our first prospect meetings.

In order to get to know our clients, we have more than sixty open-ended questions that help us understand our clients' bigger picture. They are a guide more than a list. Sometimes they answer several questions with one answer, and others don't apply. Often, their answers spur follow-up questions.

A legal pad and a pen keep us from staring at a computer screen while we're with them, and we do everything we can to let them know we're genuinely interested in everything they have to say. After an hour or more, we ask the potential client if we missed anything. Most have never had such an in-depth interview. No one has ever asked them those kinds of questions before, especially in a planning session.

By the end of our meeting, we know more about them than anyone else in their life. At the same time, we let them know I'm aware they're interviewing us, too. They get to decide if they want to use our services.

Clients usually find themselves so surprised by the end of the conversation that the Trust Gap immediately begins to narrow. They feel heard and understood. The questions not only demonstrate that we're interested, but the answers also give us the information we need to offer pertinent advice. Plus, we often refer to the details they shared to explain why we're making recommendations. Because they sense our team really wants to get to know them, they typically put their confidence in our practice quickly.

What Makes for a Great Question

Some people ask what kind of questions we ask that close the Trust Gap so quickly. Many have nothing to do with their finances. Instead, they just let us get to know them. The list has more than five dozen questions, and time doesn't always allow us to get into all of them in the first session; however, within a few months, we learn all we can from our clients. Here are a few of the more unusual questions:

- What do you do on the weekends?
- What do you do in your free time?
- What's your favorite movie?
- Do you have pets?
- Where did you go to college?
- Do you have any health concerns?
- Do you have any charitable causes you like to support?
- What would an ideal weekend look like?
- What's your favorite sports team, movie, music, author ...?

We also ask a question inspired by Strategic Coach: If we were meeting here three years from today, and you were to look back over those three years to today, what has to have happened in your life for you to feel happy about your progress?

Asking about things unrelated to your business but important to your client will make you stand out. Recently, a waiter at a restaurant asked if we were originally from that area. It turns out he was from the same area in New Jersey that we came from. We had frequented many of the same places. We definitely clicked, and the tip reflected it. Not only that, when we return, we request that waiter, and he treats us like royalty. We've even had people at neighboring tables as if we were famous because he gives us such outstanding service.

My staff knows more pets' names than I would have ever imagined. One client who lived in Hawaii and has since passed used to send us pictures of his cat on a regular basis.

These questions give us opportunities to relate and make connections. Our interest in them outside our business makes us more attractive and more referable. Think about how many businesses you have dealt with. How close are they willing to get to their clients?

Authenticity Narrows the Trust Gap

Nothing closes the Trust Gap more than the client being able to sense that you authentically care about them. That's why we emphasize always Be Genuine and Generous[IP]. The "genuine" is about kindness and following the golden rule. The "generous" is about being free with the resources you have available to you, including time, knowledge, patience, wisdom, and hard work. This short phrase drives our meetings, our interactions, and everything we do on a daily basis.

Asking great questions and listening helps our prospects and clients see we are genuine. We all know what it feels like when someone tries to butter us up. Think about the last salesperson who gave you the impression they were only interested in the sale.

If you want current and prospective clients to see that your interest is authentic, save some questions for after you finish talking business. Perhaps your client told you about her mother's health problems the last time you met. It will mean a lot if you end the conversation by asking about her.

One of my early mentors and great friends, Paul Fahrenwald, taught me to set aside the final couple minutes of our meeting to ask about the things the person mentioned the last time we met. This removes any appearance of trying to look impressive. When you start the conversation with these questions, the client might think you're trying to influence their decisions; however, the same discussion at the end leaves no room for speculation about your motives. Paul said ending the meeting this way tells the client you care so much about them you don't want to rush on to the next thing.

Part of being genuine and generous includes generosity with your time. We typically hear the word "generous" and immediately think of giving away money. While it can involve money, it does not need to. We try to be generous with our patience, our kindness, our advice, and our listening. There are so many ways to be generous, and often, these are the forms of generosity that prove to others that we truly care for them.

The way we treat people causes them to love us as much as we love them. We often say, "When you choose to work with us, you are family to us." You'll know you've really closed the Trust Gap when the client takes time to ask you about your family. When you care for them, you'll quickly become one of the most important people in their lives. In our office, we find that those who have been with us even a short time feel like family and treat us as such.

Implementation

To see how well your business implements Principle Two, think about your last few conversations.

- Who talked more, you or the person you were with?

- In your business or relationships, if you used a scale of 1–10 with one being very little and ten being a great deal, how much do you think people trust you?
- What kind of questions do you typically ask when you're having a conversation?

Principle Three

Your Interest in Others Makes You More Interesting

I HAVE BEEN fortunate enough to have learned from the best. My mother's life reinforces the idea of Principle Three: Your Interest in Others Makes You More Interesting. My mother always focuses on others first. Everyone who calls her knows they'll be on the phone for a while because she will ask question after question until she has all the information she needs to provide the appropriate support. Her genuine interest has a significant impact on the world around her, and while it's not a popular theory, I've learned that when you become interested in others, you suddenly become interesting.

I first heard the principle in a Dale Carnegie class that included his book How to Win Friends and Influence People. He said, "You can make more friends in two months by becoming interested in other people than in two years by trying to get other people interested in you."

In a workshop I attended years ago, Lee Brower, my personal coach and great friend from Strategic Coach, pointed out that social media has convinced people they need to find ways to look more interesting. Most posts point us to the person or personality and highlight the best aspects of their life. The idea permeates advertising and the news. "Look how interesting I am" is the message of the twenty-first century.

Without even trying, my mother practices active listening, the art of letting the other person talk without getting distracted or worrying about how you'll answer. She doesn't do it to impress; she genuinely cares, and people can sense it. My mom's quest to be more interested than interesting has made her a trusted confidante to many.

Making sure clients and prospects know you're interested in everything about them is the first step in closing the Trust Gap. The examples of my mother and grandmother make a good foundation. When we learn to ask good questions and listen because we are authentically interested in the other person's answers, we will be amazed at how quickly the gap shrinks.

Businesses that bridge the Trust Gap reach a similar level of confidence. It moves them from average to excellent, from reliable to referable. Many surveys list trust as a top reason people make purchases. One study, in particular, identifies this quality as the number one consideration. Those questioned said trusting a company based on reputation, reliability, and recommendations is more important than the quality of the product.[1]

Learning Not to Interrupt

Another aspect of listening that closes the Trust Gap also falls under the category of good manners. A great listener learns not to interrupt.

I hate it when I get so excited about a topic that I jump in and share my thoughts before the other person has a chance to finish. I don't mean to, but it happens sometimes. And unfortunately, it makes it look like I'm more interested in what I have to say than what the other person is saying.

If you talk to people on a regular basis, you probably interrupt without even realizing it. Sometimes we think the other person is done, and other times we just need to give our two cents. Generally, it happens because instead of actively listening, we're busy figuring out what to say next. When we think ahead, trying to make ourselves interesting, we forget to be interested and miss essential details in the conversation. Whatever the reason, learning to actively listen, pause, and let people process their thoughts in silence proves invaluable in every relationship.

Empathy Means Holding Their Hurt in Your Heart

When we learn to immerse ourselves in being interested in others, we start to experience empathy. Some people naturally feel others' pain. When their friends celebrate, they feel extreme joy. They constantly walk in someone else's proverbial shoes. These empaths hold their friends' hurts and joys in their hearts without even trying.

But can this inherent trait be learned?

I say yes.

Learning to listen puts us on the path to empathy.

To feel what others feel, you have to hear their pain. As you learn the art of slowing down, asking good questions, and listening, your ability to feel and show empathy will grow.

As I've mentioned, our clients become like family. The more we know about them, the easier it is to feel what they've experienced and be deeply touched by their concerns. And candidly, empathy can derail your meetings from time to time. Because we care about what's happening in their lives, if a client has a concern that's unrelated to their accounts, we want to hear it.

Not long ago, I put my meeting agenda aside because the client had been robbed. In the middle of the night, someone had broken into his office. He just needed someone to be willing to lend an ear. Empathy knew this current situation was raw. It needed attention. I held his pain, felt his anger, and gave him space to get it off his chest.

The more you practice being interested without interruption and holding the clients' hurts in your heart, the more natural it will become, and the more interesting and attractive working with you will be.

Implementation

- How important is Principle Three in your business and relationships? Do you spend more time being interested or trying to be interesting?
- How often do you interrupt? If you're not sure, pay attention in the next conversation, and take a count.
- What questions could you add to your conversations to become more interested?
- What strategies could you implement to help you stop interrupting? Could you listen more intently or write down some memorable facts from what the other person says to help you pay more attention? Would it help to count to three before you fill the gap in the conversation?
- How do you feel when you have to give up your agenda to talk about your client's current situation? What can you do to make sure what's important to the client gets covered in every conversation?

Principle Four

Clear Commitments and Follow-Through Close the Trust Gap

DO YOU GET as frustrated as I do when people consistently tell you they'll do something and they don't follow through? When someone arrives late to a meeting several times in a row, I start to doubt their apology. It makes me wonder, *what happens to the Trust Gap if the client can't count on me to keep my word about something as simple as a meeting time?*

Dan Sullivan says that "doing what you say you're going to do" is one of the three keys to a referable business. The communication involved in following through, as well as the confidence it builds, puts Principle Four, Clear Commitments and Follow-Through Close the Trust Gap, high on the list of things that make a referable business.

Great Processes Help You Make Clear Commitments

Our office has a list of processes that take us from introduction to final steps, no matter what we're dealing with. Whether it's client onboarding or connecting for birthdays, you'll find a process in place. Gino Wickman, author of the book *Traction* and the genius behind the Entrepreneurial Operating System® (EOS®), says, "Systemize the predictable so you can humanize the exceptional." Our processes let us systemize; these principles encourage us to humanize.

The number one secret to the success of our written procedures is implementing the eight principles in this book. Likewise, the processes help us practice the principles more effectively, and none more so than making clear commitments and ensuring we follow through.

Clear Commitments require clear communication, the root of any attempt to systemize. By putting our steps into an unmistakable process, we exponentially increase our success. Every time we hang up the phone or a client leaves the office, we believe they should know exactly what steps we will take next. Clearly communicating our intentions keeps our team from waking up at three in the morning thinking, "I forgot to call about that insurance quote again. I have to remember to do that tomorrow." Plus, it prevents our clients from wondering whose job it is to follow up. We don't want that for anyone.

Put Follow-Through in All Your Processes

Through the years, I've learned a great deal from Don Connelly's newsletters and podcasts. His advice was and is invaluable. He's the one who first told me that people don't necessarily remember what you do for them, but they do remember that you care. My friend and mentor continues to serve as a coach to advisors nationwide and delivers his wisdom weekly on his Substack blog. It's Don who inspired our practice's follow-through process.

Follow-up is a common business process; we used to have one. However, because of Don's inspiration, we changed to a follow-through process. A follow-up strategy leaves a message on an answering machine to check on things after the transaction is completed. A follow-through process means someone takes personal responsibility for the project, walking through every task along the way. Follow-through also takes communication to the next level.

For instance, take something as simple as a money transfer. Someone in our office speaks with the client the day of the request, and when the transfer has been initiated, so the client knows to watch for it and give us a call if it doesn't go through smoothly.

When we give an insurance quote, we know the worst thing we can do for the client is send the quote and wait for their response. They don't need another thing on their to-do list. So, before we send the information, we schedule a meeting for the following week. If the client doesn't have a date available, we add a phone call appointment to our calendar. Someone on our staff gets in touch in the week following to set up a meeting or answer questions. We explain the process to the client so they expect it.

We tell them, "Instead of adding something else to your to-do list, would you like to schedule a meeting to talk about this quote next week, or would it be better if I called you in a few days to set something up or answer your questions?"

Know Your Limitations

Clear commitments also mean you don't overcommit. When people make promises they know they can't deliver on, simply because they think it will make them look good, they end up disappointing someone. When you build in time for the unexpected, you never have to call the client and tell them you're running behind. No one minds hearing that you finished their project early.

I've heard it said that overcommitting is the same as not committing at all. You defeat yourself before you begin. Clients appreciate an "under-promise/over-deliver" philosophy. They grow to know they can count on you.

I'm great at connecting with people, but my to-do list would get out of hand if I took on every follow-through myself. Knowing and acknowledging this limitation allows me to better serve my clients.

When we know a phone call needs to be made after a quote has been sent or a transaction completed, one of us puts it on our calendar as an appointment rather than as a task. We assign a specific person so no one wonders who is responsible, and that person follows through.

These defined calendar dates give the follow-through status. Even if all the task needs is a five-minute phone call, the space on the calendar keeps it from being forgotten or left as an afterthought. Scheduling tasks gives them the priority they deserve.

Unfortunately, sometimes things get held up. Projects take longer than expected, outside forces push the deadlines, and unforeseen things happen. People understand. However, we take the extra step to give them a call or send an email so they aren't left wondering. And when those pauses happen frequently, we know it's time to revisit our processes or add to our team.

Adhering to this principle requires putting processes in place to make sure nothing falls through the cracks. Our process also lets my team sleep well at night. They don't wake up wondering what they forgot or have a nightmare about a task they pushed to the back burner. Without intentionality, you might look back through old appointments or start cleaning up your email folder and discover you missed checking on someone.

Show up on Time

Our culture has trained us to accept the fact that planes take off late, and we have to sit in doctors' offices thirty minutes past our appointment time. This means when you implement Principle Four, you will automatically impress people.

Dan Sullivan's final rule for having a referable business is "Always show up on time," and I'm passionate about this. If you think about it, being on time is really just good manners, and it tells people they're important.

Whether it's a traditional meeting, a Zoom meeting, or a phone call, we insist on punctuality. When we tell someone we're going to call at two in the afternoon, we don't call a minute before or after. Our clients are busy. We don't want to interrupt what they're doing before our scheduled call, and we don't want to be late. People know they can set their clocks by my team. And if we're even one minute late, we apologize. Time is valuable, whether it's mine or the person on my schedule.

We also try to make our commitment and communication clear at the beginning of the meeting. As we start, we tell the client what time we plan to finish. This allows us to respect the people in our next meeting and lets the client know we're not going to hold them prisoner past our meeting time. We don't want to be the people who steal minutes from other vital parts of their day.

For ten years, from 2010 to 2020, I wore the hat of regional leader over several dozen offices in the Dallas-Fort Worth area. Even today, I mentor dozens of advisors at a quarterly Zoom meeting. People know that when I'm in charge, the meeting or conference will begin on time, whether they are there or not. I don't play the "let's wait a few minutes in case a few more people show up" game. I feel like this is disrespectful to all those who showed up on time, and delaying teaches people that arriving late is acceptable. It simply is not. In my Zoom meetings, I often remind them I am committed to starting on time because doing so shows respect, and punctuality is a referable habit.

Think about how you feel when people consistently show up late to appointments or events. This kind of behavior sends a subliminal message. Your time isn't as important as mine. This meeting wasn't a priority.

Some businesspeople use the "another meeting ran over" excuse, but that tells the client that the person before them is more valuable to your business.

Every action sends a message. What do you say with your brand of punctuality?

The Problem with Excuses

People who haven't prioritized clear commitments and follow through will have a list of reasons they miss deadlines, run late for meetings, and neglect responsibilities. To become referable, we have to distinguish between reasons and excuses, because sadly, the majority of their list falls in the second category.

What happens if my team tells someone we will send a check by a specific date, and it doesn't arrive? No reason we invent will be enough to help the client pay their bills. And when the "reasons" become a habit, the delays become acceptable. You end up continually playing catch-up, and it affects the morale of the entire office. Your staff becomes reactive instead of responsive. Clients become disgruntled, and everyone is on edge, waiting for the next complaint to come in.

If you want to be a referable person or you want a referable business, you need follow-through processes in place that make excuses unacceptable.

When Things Go Wrong

As hard as we try to always follow through, be on time, and adhere to our processes perfectly, not everything ends perfectly. Sometimes, unexpected and unavoidable situations occur. People get sick, computers fail, telephones go down, and mistakes happen. A big part of follow-through is taking responsibility early and letting people know when you aren't going to be able to keep your commitment.

Staying referable means owning the problem and staying on top of the solution. We've all dealt with those businesses that make a mistake, promise to never let it happen again, and then repeat the annoying procedure again and again.

In our office, we start with apologies and explain that we didn't mean for the error to happen. We express appreciation for their patience, and we make it right. If the client brought the problem to our attention, we thank them for giving us an opportunity to fix it. We're blessed to have understanding clients. Because so many of them have been referred to us by kind people who appreciate us, they are very understanding that things might occasionally go awry.

Regardless of their graciousness, we revisit our processes to identify the point where we fell short. Did someone try to take a shortcut, or do we need to revise the process to address the failure?

Mistakes happen, but taking ownership and correcting the problem will quickly close the Trust Gap. Most people don't expect perfection all the time. They appreciate the authenticity and honesty the imperfection reveals. In a world where everyone tries to make excuses and pass blame, when you take responsibility, you will stand out.

Implementation

- How do you implement Principle Four? What written processes do you have in place that make commitments to ensure the project never falls through the cracks?
- What processes do you have in place to make up for your limitations?
- How often do you show up late? What can you do to make sure you are always punctual?
- How do you handle mistakes? What is your procedure? Do you allow for excuses?

Principle Five

Find Unique Ways to Reach Out to Let People Know You Care

WHEN WAS THE last time you received a handwritten note in the mail or someone took the time to call you rather than text? Today, we get all our news through email and texts. So, when people take an envelope out of the mailbox with their address written in ink and a stamp in the corner, it has special meaning. Principle Five invites us to find unique ways to reach out to our clients. We could send notes by email, but would that make us stand out?

The Simplest Ways to Reach Out

One of the first ways we reach out is shortly after someone decides to be our client. We send a handwritten thank-you note to let the client know how much we appreciate their trust in us with their portfolio. Our team also sends holiday cards; however, because we like to stand out, we don't send them in December. Everyone does that. Instead, we send Thanksgiving cards. People get flooded with cards in the last few weeks of the year, but ours is likely the only Thanksgiving card they receive.

The Thanksgiving card feels more appropriate anyway. Since it's a time of gratitude and appreciation, it's the perfect time for us to remind our clients how grateful we are to know them and how privileged we feel to have them in our lives.

We use the annual review as another simple way to let people know how important they are to us. As we close the meeting, we try to say, "I just want to pause before we wrap things up. We appreciate that you've stayed with us for so many years, and I want you to know that not a day goes by that I take that for granted. It's such a pleasure to work with you. I hope you know how much we love working with you and your family."

Using the word "love" is unheard of in business today, and we probably don't say it enough. But we truly do love our clients, and we want them to know it. So, whenever the opportunity presents itself, and whenever it's appropriate, we try to let them know how much we care for and love their family.

We do something a bit unusual around birthdays, too. Many places send birthday and anniversary cards. It's a tremendous practice. But how much more do you think it stands out when our clients receive a phone call that avoids any discussion of business on their special day? Of course, if the client has questions, we will definitely answer them; however, we want the person to know they are more important than the business we do with them. Our goal is to simply make their day brighter.

Many years ago, I called a long-time client to wish him happy birthday. When he answered, and I gave him the birthday wishes, he laughed out loud. "My own brother doesn't call me to wish me happy birthday!" Some of our longtime clients have come to expect that call. I think they would be disappointed if we ever stopped doing it.

The Client Care Cycle[IP]

One of the easiest ways we maintain contact is an idea I got from my friends Tom Hosey and Dustin Smith, who helped me when I started in business. They shared their contact process with me, and we adapted it into the Client Care Cycle. This process ensures no one falls through the cracks.

Every quarter, our team divides the number of clients by the number of working days during that three-month period to create a daily contact list. For instance, if we have 300 clients and 60 working days, we plan to contact five people each day, so we're reaching out to everyone quarterly.

Other offices have adopted this system and use a variety of sorting methods, but we simply sort alphabetically. Every day, the person in charge of the list creates a sheet for me. It includes the names of the five individuals or families we want our team to contact that day, as well as the dates of our last conversation and their next annual review. Beside every name, I put a 1, 2, 3, or X to communicate with our wonderful team how they should reach out:

- **X** – We've talked to them recently, so we don't need to contact them this quarter. We understand that a call saying, "I'm just checking in," can be very annoying in this culture of telemarketing calls. If we're going to contact a client, we want to be sure to provide value.
- **1** – Please make a check-in call. Someone on the team calls and provides value. Sometimes we check beneficiaries or their trusted contacts. Other times, the team will send them a particular report that would be of interest to them. We also use this as a follow-through call when necessary.
- **2** – Please call and set up a ten-minute phone meeting with this client and put it on Dave's calendar. When we

add these meetings to the calendar, it saves everyone time. I don't catch them at an inconvenient time, and there's less back and forth. Knowing I'm going to call, the client can be prepared if there's information we need.

- **3** – Please call and set up a forty-five-minute meeting with this client and put it on Dave's calendar. We need to go over something on their account.

With our team taking the lead, this practice takes me just a few minutes a day; however, it constantly puts our clients' accounts in front of us so we can keep on top of things and avoid overlooking people who skip an annual review or don't reach out to us often. The Client Care Cycle means nothing ever stretches longer than three months. It keeps us from being reactive because so often a client was going to reach out to us anyway. It ends up being a time saver for everybody.

Yes, there are many Customer Relationship Management software programs that could assist you in this endeavor; however, we've tried them, and going in alphabetical order with a paper system works better for us.

Thank You for the Referral

We also use a less recognized excuse for contact. In fact, I've asked several colleagues if they use this strategy and haven't found one yet who does.

First, we send a thank-you note to clients when they refer someone, even if their referral never calls us back or does business with us. This is tremendously important to our entire team. But what's more unusual is that we often express thanks for referrals after a year or two or five or twenty.

We have many clients who have sent multiple people they care about our way. Whenever we have an opportunity, we thank them. Sometimes an annual review will remind us of the referral. It's a perfect excuse to reach out. "We just met with the Smiths again this year. Thanks so much for sending them our way twenty-five years ago. They are a joy just like you are."

The front-end thank you is a must, but shouldn't we also continually express our gratitude to our clients for referring their friends? They deserve to be appreciated after one year, after five years, after ten years, and beyond. When they hear the thank you a decade later, it proves we meant it when we said, "I'll never forget what you did for us."

Through the Good Times and the Bad

As I mentioned, we use every phone call and meeting to learn all we can about our clients. Some conversations reveal good or bad things happening in their lives. Each one allows us to demonstrate empathy and remind the client we are genuinely interested in their lives.

Whether it's a death in the family or a serious health issue, we want the client to know they are in our thoughts. We also want to celebrate their joys—births, graduations, and new jobs, for example. When a family is facing more than one life-changing event simultaneously, we don't combine our empathy or gratitude. If they receive a cancer diagnosis and news of a death in the family the same week as their child graduates from college, we send three cards. Many times, we serve multiple generations. If so, we reach out to every party affected.

When there hasn't been an obvious way to Be Genuine and Generous through difficult times, we find new ways. During the 2020 pandemic, my friend Mike Scoma came up with an amazing way to show clients how much he appreciated them. Since no one could leave their houses, Mike took his clients on a virtual tour of Rome. His idea spread across our company quickly, including our office.

There was no sales pitch involved. It was simply a gift for our clients in the middle of a difficult time. Since then, we've taken them back to Rome, Barcelona, Sicily, and Prague at Christmas. At the end of the Barcelona tour, I asked our guide to talk about the special foods Spain is known for, as well as tips on wine we might be able to find here in the United States. The clients loved it. We received so much positive feedback from doing these types of events, which is tremendous, especially based on how little effort it takes to give back to our clients in this way.

We have found other ways to leverage video conferencing technology, especially during times of uncertainty. For example, when the market is in a correction, we will host an information session where we bring on an expert in the field as a special guest. Together, we provide a report with information and assurances that our clients aren't hearing from the media. The media is in the business of keeping people anxious. We try to put things in perspective to mitigate that anxiety. Even if our clients choose not to attend these sessions, they know we are thinking about them. Those who do attend appreciate that we spent the time to give them clarity on what's happening in the world and how it affects their financial future.

We build these practices into our processes, but the more you care about your clients and become genuinely interested in them, the easier it will be for you to naturally see these opportunities to reach out.

Implementation

Principle Five invites you to be creative in increasing communication with your clients.

- In what ways do you already reach out to your clients beyond reviews and sales?
- What creative ways could you add to reach out to your clients or customers?

Principle Six

Shortcuts Undermine the Long Game

HOW LONG WOULD you like to keep your clients? Retention means you can build your business instead of replacing revenue that leaves. And if clients keep coming back because they feel appreciated and respected, referrals will become the primary way you grow your business. Business leaders who ignore this long-term perspective and focus on today have to work ten times harder to maintain their client count. Growth will be impossible.

Shortcuts Start with a Scarcity Mindset

Principle Six reminds us that Shortcuts Undermine the Long Game; still, cutting corners has become a business norm. Many shortcuts look attractive because they offer fast money. The scarcity mindset sees a quick buck and jumps on it without weighing how it will affect clients or their team. It's not that every one of these decisions will prove detrimental; it's the shortcut mentality that produces them that can be dangerous. It might be the number one killer of a narrow Trust Gap.

An abundant mindset wants the best for everyone. The scarcity mindset protects what's mine. Looking inward will never find what's best for anyone—not you, and certainly not the client. And if you continue to look inward, clients will eventually sense it and look for someone who has their best interests in mind.

Sometimes we sit with clients who hesitate before finalizing a decision. This happens when the situation is a bit more complex than usual, or the client is entering into a world they've never experienced before. You might have discussed the decision previously and have everything one hundred percent ready to go, yet you can sense the client doesn't feel certainty.

It's tempting to try to talk them into it, but that's the time to step back and give the client permission to think about it for a week or ask more questions. The abundance mindset wants the client to feel confident about their decision.

We've worked with prospects who really needed a financial advisor. They had a nice-sized bank account and could have benefited from a financial plan. But many times, if it's the first time they've invested, we hear the hesitancy in their voice. When that happens, I stop the meeting. "Let's table this for today and schedule for next week. I think it's starting to get a bit overwhelming, and I want you to feel completely comfortable with whatever we decide."

When you find yourself rushing a client into a decision, you can bet the scarcity mindset has entered. Scarcity and shortcuts don't allow space for digesting and contemplating. An abundance mindset sees the bigger picture. It works on the client's timeline, so they feel comfortable rather than pressured. In the long game, this builds trust.

No Need for Shortcuts

One of the best features of these principles and processes is their built-in growth system. When you always have new clients coming in through referrals, you'll feel less pressure to close deals. Slow revenue months, quotas, and income minimums can push people toward these shortcuts, and even if you don't mean for them to, they'll eventually take over your culture.

Car dealers have the worst stereotype for high-pressure, quota-driven sales. I've been in those offices where they wanted me to sit for hours while they tried to convince me the vehicle was right for me. No matter how many times I say, "I'm not ready yet" or "I don't really want to talk to your manager," the salesperson presses.

Do you really want to return to these places? And will you tell your friends to buy a car there?

Shortcuts Steal Your Integrity

Every shortcut steals from someone or something—your client, your team, your time, even you. When you undermine your long game like this, you rob yourself.

For some people, the shortcut starts innocently. "I'll just drop it off. I was going to be driving by your house anyway."

That sounds impressive and kind, but if you weren't going to drive by their house, the little fib will make it easier to tell a bigger fib next time. Why do some feel obliged to add the second sentence when offering to drop it off would have been enough?

Young businesspeople sometimes want to sound experienced. They'll share a story that actually happened to one of their managers to elevate themselves. The same story with an acknowledgment that it originated from someplace else will make a greater impression.

People who take shortcuts will also often take credit for other people's work. It takes an extra moment or two to let people know you're sharing someone else's thoughts. Some people enjoy the attention great ideas bring. Others are too lazy to find out who to credit. However, integrity is an extremely referable trait.

I'm often asked to give talks at my company, and as best I can, I always give credit for the ideas that I have learned from someone else. Likewise, even though I've adapted it to make it my own, when I share the Client Care Cycle, I give credit to the people who gave me the idea. When you introduce another's concept, start the description with a phrase as simple as, "A colleague showed me..." or "I read something..." This allows you to maintain your reputation. Sometimes, people will be in a situation where they are sharing ideas in front of a group, and they neglect to name the source of these ideas. Sadly, this kind of shortcut robs you of respect in venues where they've heard the idea from the originator. People who know you claimed someone else's idea wonder if they can believe you about other things you share.

When you give credit where credit is due, you gain respect. You won't need to give every bit of information and pass along credit in every situation. But when you're in a more formal setting or a place where you're trying to close the Trust Gap, it's imperative. One of the things I've attempted to do throughout this book is to acknowledge when someone has influenced me or contributed to my process.

Early in my career, I didn't recognize how vital this principle is. Looking back, I regret those times when I inadvertently took credit that wasn't mine. I still don't get it right all the time, but I appreciate great ideas, and I want to share them and their source whenever possible. I want you to trust and respect me, so I'll never let that millisecond shortcut steal my integrity.

Implementation

This is the perfect time to review your processes and policies. Checkpoints and boundaries help ensure you aren't running your business from a scarcity mindset. Use these questions to determine whether you're successfully carrying out Principle Six or letting shortcuts steal from you.

- Do you always keep the clients' best interests and the long game in mind?
- Does everyone on your team know shortcuts are not an option? Do they expect you to call them out if they start to take a shortcut?
- Do members of your team have permission to question your decision if it looks like you might be taking a shortcut—even if you're not intentionally trying to shortcut anything?

Principle Seven

Take Care of Your Team, and Your Team Will Take Care of You

<hr>

WE LOVE OUR clients, and we want to treat every person who walks through our doors in a way that demonstrates this caring. But I don't want to treat my clients better than I do my team. I feel blessed to work with the people in our company. We all love each other and enjoy working together. That's why Principles Seven and Eight encompass the people who share your office. When you Take Care of Your Team, Your Team Will Take Care of You. Many, if not all, the principles you've already read should extend to your team.

I couldn't do everything I do without my current team of Karen, Kendra, Ben, Karen, Matt, and so many others who have carried out these principles with us through the years. These people deserve to be treated every bit as well as our best clients. I always want to say please and thank you when I'm talking with them. We have built a culture where we truly enjoy being with one another. During the COVID pandemic, any one of us could have worked from home, but since our industry was deemed essential, and nothing kept us out of the office, we chose to work together. We're genuinely interested in each other's lives, and we treat one another with the same respect we treat our clients. Nothing builds a tremendous team faster than showing appreciation every single day, and when you create written processes around the way you want to treat your team, you reinforce their importance in your life.

Expenses Versus Investments

Appreciation starts with shifting your mindset around the cost of your team. Every business owner has to look at their profitability statement regularly. We all have unavoidable expenses as well as those we can trim to increase profit. Many business leaders make the mistake of putting their employees on the list of expenses.

Referable businesses see every expense related to their team as an investment. We view salaries, bonuses, and incentives as investments. The return on what I do for my team can't be measured. In fact, the more I do, the more that comes back to me.

Though I did it occasionally prior to 2020, during the pandemic, I started bringing in lunch on a regular basis to thank them for coming into the office when they could have stayed home. One evening every week, I text everyone to let them know they don't need to pack a lunch the next day. They never know which day it will be, but it has become one way for me to show my gratitude. Most business owners and the IRS might look at it as an expense, but I consider it an investment.

One part of investing in your team that some business people miss is giving regular bonuses that grow as the business grows. Don't be afraid to give your team a fair percentage. It's typical for my team's bonuses to exceed their salaries. That might scare some entrepreneurs; however, I'm happy when it happens. They've earned it, and bigger bonuses mean the company is growing.

Even our celebrations become investments. My wife and I love to celebrate with our team. When things are going well in the business—and because of my team, they're always going well—we create special experiences to celebrate even the smallest things. We usually take everyone out for our holiday dinner, but one year, to make the celebration even more special, we hired a Hibachi chef, Chef Han, to come to our house. Everyone on the team came with their plus-one. We had such a good time, we've done it multiple times!

Personal Development

We also invest in personal development. Our industry requires a great deal of continuing education, but I encourage my team to pursue any type of training that will help them do their jobs better. I hired a sales coach to work with Kendra, my associate financial advisor, and invested thousands in helping her and Ben become better salespeople. This kind of investment increases their capabilities as well as their confidence.

My associate financial advisor is taking advantage of the coaching, and she's become like my right arm. She can do everything I can do. Some owners would discourage that kind of advancement. There's a chance, because I invest in her, she'll eventually reach the point where she'll branch out on her own. And if she does, I will be proud.

Referable businesses don't live in that kind of fear. I've actually had two assistants grow and leave. Brooke and Karli aren't competitors; they are colleagues. I couldn't be happier or prouder of their accomplishments. I could have hindered their development and tried to keep them close, but they were destined to run their own offices someday. And because I always wanted the best for them, we're all still good friends. Without developing them, our team wouldn't have been as attractive to my current teammates.

By viewing every penny I spend on my team as an investment, the company grows. It opens doors and creates a loving family-type atmosphere. In fact, because of the way our parent company has restructured since my first two assistants left, my current assistant could easily transition into a financial advisor who goes out and finds her own clients from this office. And the team dynamic we've built creates a space where she'll want to do that.

Taking care of your team doesn't build competition; it builds connections, company capabilities, and client confidence. Our clients love watching us develop the next generation and letting them shine. Brooke and Karli set out on their own years ago; still, a few people come in and ask how they are doing. They know we keep in touch and feel like they had a part in her growth. Those clients are as proud of her as I am.

The more I invest in my team, the better our practice does. When your clients see you investing in your team and allowing them to grow, they recognize you as the kind of people who want the best for everyone. They assume if you're working for the best interests of your team, you must be working in their best interest, too.

The Referable Framework Will Take Your Team to the Next Level

The first six principles work in every relationship, including your team. When we implement the golden rule in our workplace, we make our team feel loved and highly valued. Everything we've talked about so far will help us create a team that takes care of our clients and builds our business.

For instance, though I don't mean to, sometimes my team must think I'm trying to make them read my mind. When I write notes, I know exactly what I mean. However, because I'm wired to constantly work three steps ahead, it's easy for me to leave out pertinent details. In our office, clear communication includes my team having permission to slow me down to provide clarity. I don't expect them to guess my intentions. I take responsibility for the way I work, and I appreciate it when they come up to me and joke, "I'm sure you know what this means, but my mind-reading skills haven't fully developed yet."

My team also enjoys notes of appreciation. When I'm out of the office for an extended period of time, I will sometimes send a note to let them know how much I appreciate being able to go on vacation or attend a conference and not worry about the business while I'm away. I have complete confidence that everything will be handled and taken care of. Investing in them, providing development opportunities, and having processes in place so they know exactly what I would do allows them to run the office without me, and I don't take that luxury for granted.

Just like you don't want to take shortcuts with your clients, you don't want to take them with your team. They shouldn't feel pressured to choose between family and work, and we should never ask them to make a career decision on short notice. Unless it's required for compliance, training needs to take their personal situations into consideration. Does their family life allow them to travel out of town right now? Do they have the bandwidth to study and keep their outside-of-work commitments?

Keeping an investment mindset will help you keep the long game in view. You spend time training, and your clients grow close to your team. You want to keep them. We try to treat our team with love, which includes looking at how our policies affect them and their families. It includes the way we handle our team members' doctor appointments, the time they need to take care of important family matters, and the bonuses we give. I encourage you to ask often, "What do we do to show our team how vital they are?"

Implementation

Taking care of your team means seeing them as an investment rather than an expense. Your spending habits will reveal how well you've implemented Principle Seven:

- Do you invest in personal development for your team?
- Do you use the first six principles to create an inviting workspace for your team?
    - Do you use please, thank you, and other manners with your team?
    - Do you listen to your team and stay authentic with them?
    - Are you authentically interested in every part of their lives?
    - Do you keep commitments with your team as if they were your most important client?
    - Do you find reasons to reach out to your team members to encourage them and show your appreciation?
- What do you do to make sure your team understands how important they are to the success of your business?

Principle Eight

Communicate Compliments; Keep Complaints

WHEN OUR CLIENT Craig texted, *We need to talk*, I called him right away. "Hi, Craig."

"Hi, Dave, I need to talk to you about your assistant," he said.

My heart dropped. I couldn't think of anything Kendra could have done, but he called my personal phone for business. It had to be serious.

"I knew if I called the office, I wouldn't get you first, and I really wanted to tell you this personally."

I stayed silent, waiting for the worst.

"Kendra always does such an amazing job. She's been a tremendous help to me and my wife. Over and over again, she goes above and beyond. I just thought you should know."

I should have known it couldn't be a complaint. He just caught me off guard by calling my cell.

As soon as I got off the phone, I headed over to Kendra's office and told her the entire conversation.

Share the Compliments

I get compliments like this all the time. I shouldn't have been surprised. Almost daily, someone praises an individual or the entire team. And every time I get one, I walk out of my office and relay the message personally. I don't send an email or a memo. I go out and find the person as quickly as I can and share the good news. We love practicing Principle Eight: Communicate Compliments, Keep Complaints.

Teams need the kind of reinforcement compliments bring. I want them to know people are talking about them—and in a good way! I always end the conversation by telling them how much I appreciate them and the work they did that created the compliment.

Keep Criticism to Yourself

In *Good to Great*, author Jim Collins says top-level leaders look out the window and "attribute success to factors outside themselves," like their team, and they look in the mirror to take responsibility for criticism.

We don't get many complaints, but when we do, I can generally track it back to a process that needs tightening or some training I haven't provided. Sometimes I haven't communicated properly, or I didn't tell the person what to say. Regardless of where the complaint originated, I take responsibility.

That doesn't mean I dismiss it. We still have to address it as a team, but we don't try to place blame. Instead, we discuss what went wrong and explore how this same situation can be prevented in the future. I tell the team, "We all do dumb things, but smart people don't do the same dumb things twice."

Is this something that slipped through the cracks, or did the process produce the crack? Was it a follow-through issue?

Getting to the root and fixing the issue empowers your team for the next time a similar situation arises.

I think clients appreciate it when I take blame. They feel more confident in the leadership, and it makes them want to partner with us. On top of that, I invite the team to tell me when I've done something wrong. I can't improve if no one ever tells me when I could do it differently.

The best athletes hire coaches for a reason. They don't need someone to tell them how wonderful they are; they look for someone who can critique their game and tell them what they're doing wrong. They grow through advice and constructive criticism.

Build Team Confidence

When we resist placing blame, we also empower our team to take action. They don't have to be afraid to take chances, make decisions, or own a project. They know if something goes wrong, we'll fix it as a team; they aren't alone.

Fortunately, because we've put processes in place and I take care of the team, the compliments outweigh the complaints by a long shot. We rarely have complaints. And we choose to look at them as invitations, actionable advice to help us move forward and grow, as we focus on the compliments. The things you focus on become amplified. When you keep your eyes on what you've done right, you're more likely to repeat that behavior.

Referable people pour into others. All the people I've mentioned make up just a few who have contributed to my success, and now I feel privileged to pour into my team as well as neighboring advisors who need help getting started. If you take care of your team and pour into them, you will have an unstoppable culture that attracts clients and invites referrals without saying a word. Take the advice of my dad and Mister Rogers and be kind to your team.

Implementation

Principle Eight will keep morale high and give you excuses to lift your team up.

- Do you have processes to remind you how you want your team to be treated?
- What is your process for sharing compliments?
- How do you process complaints?

Bonus: Your Team Is Bigger than You Think (Especially If You Thought You Didn't Have One)

DID YOU SKIP the last two chapters because you don't have a team? If so, I'm going to challenge you to go back and read. And if you already read those two chapters, I want to push you to recognize every person who makes your business great.

I know I saved the chapters on how teams create a referable business till last, but that doesn't mean these people should be treated as less vital. In fact, your team might be the most critical ingredient in your referable business. And whether you realize it or not, even solopreneurs and lone-ranger business leaders have a team. It's a part of the company some long-time business people overlook.

Who Are the People Who Support You?

Every person has a network that supports them in their endeavors. If you're young, it might be your parents. And nearly everyone has friends who will come out on opening day just to be "the crowd" or turn themselves into your marketing department by sharing posts on social media. Those who have a brick-and-mortar business probably enlisted a few of these friends to do some heavy lifting before their launch.

If you're married, your spouse gives you support—sometimes by simply giving you space or keeping the household running while you're trying to get the business off the ground. Your children need to be treated like your team, especially if you've enlisted their help or found yourself working extra hours because you're in the first few years of making your business a reality.

Speaking of spouses, I could not have done this without Julie's support. I started with this firm the year we were married. She walked with me through those early years of building my practice and put up with me working all the hours necessary when an entrepreneur takes those first steps. She stayed home with the kids and supported me every moment along the way. Even though I have a team in my office, she's still instrumental in making this business a success.

The Service Providers on Your Team

In addition to family and friends, entrepreneurs depend on many service industries to keep the business going. What would you do without your local postal worker or FedEx® driver? Could you sustain your business without the person who installed or set up your internet? If you use a cleaning service, a plumber, or a handyman, these people are all part of your team.

Maybe you have an online business. Are you one of those solopreneurs who call the local coffee shop their "office"? Should you count the barista as a team member? Do you meet clients at the same restaurant every day? You might add that waitress who knows your order before you place it at the top of your list of team members.

I'm grateful for my firm's home office, and I try to express my appreciation every time I call. They do so much behind the scenes that our clients don't see, and I want to make sure they know their work doesn't go unnoticed.

No businessperson on planet Earth can live in a total void. Your team might be more difficult to define than mine, but acknowledging those people is no less valuable. In fact, if you have a defined in-house team, you should still consider these service providers as well as your family and friends when you make plans to take care of the people who help you get your work done. It's easy to overlook these essential pillars of our entrepreneurship, but could you really stay in business without them?

Implementation

Take time today to list these people who are not on your payroll but provide untold value to your business. Whether or not you have an internal team, these outside supporters deserve to be treated like family.

- Make a list of the people on your external team. Who helps your business run smoothly every day that most people take for granted? Do you have an outside support staff like my firm's home office? Be sure to include everyone who impacts your day-to-day operations.

- Create a defined process to thank the people on your external team list.
- How can you lift up these supporters on a regular basis?

Prodigious

Be the Business Everyone Wants to Work With

WE'VE FOUND THAT every time our clients gather, we get an inflow of introductions on the days that follow, all because of the simple things we do every day. We follow the Golden Rule and show empathy. We have a mission: Anytime someone interacts with us, we want their day to be better for it.

How do we know our strategy works—besides our customer retention and referral rate? Our parent company invites J.D. Powers to research all the firms under their umbrella, and our office typically ranks in the top for customer satisfaction rating. At a national gathering of our firm's 200 top-producing firms in North America, our office was recognized for being in the top three in customer service scores. Even more recently, we won first place for customer service in our region.

I believe these accolades stem from the fact that my entire office lives and breathes these processes every day. We also use strategies that protect what Strategic Coach calls my Unique Ability®. Your Unique Ability is what you were put on this earth to do. You do it like no one else, and when you give yourself permission to work in your Unique Ability as much as possible, you provide better service for your clients.

Because my team and I focus on staying in our Unique Ability as much as possible, we free ourselves to do what we each do best. Understanding this and making it a priority keeps us from overcommitting to things outside our areas of expertise.

Three Levels of Referability

By now, you may be wondering, *if I don't implement all eight of these principles, will I become unreferable? Could I get away with putting all but one into practice?*

I would say you could, but why would you settle for less than absolutely spectacular? There are three levels of referability. My goal is to help you get to the top level:

- **UNREFERABLE:** If you're constantly late, don't communicate, show no interest in people who do business with you, or treat people with disrespect, you've made yourself unreferable. In fact, when people bring up your business in conversation, someone probably recommends your competition.
- **REQUESTED REFERRAL:** Businesses who fall in this category are referable only if requested. These businesses may practice a few of the Eight Principles, but they typically care more about the quality of their work than the satisfaction of their customers. If someone asks who we recommend, we'll pass along the name of these businesses, but seldom do we spontaneously share the recommendation. For example, if you're a world-class surgeon, you might be able to get away with being a jerk and find yourself

with requested referrals. Some situations in our lives require the highest skill level, so we'll put up with the lack of interest or appreciation. But the majority of businesses shouldn't count on their expertise to drive referrals.

- **NATURAL REFERRALS:** Referable businesses get natural referrals because their clients constantly talk about their experience. Referable businesses come up in conversation. You might be in this category without maximizing these principles; however, the most referable businesses practice The Eight Principles of the Referable Framework and have processes in place to help them systematize their intentionality.

From the Top Down

As the leader in our practice, I know the culture of our office begins with me. If I don't put these common courtesies and intentional actions into practice, I can't expect the rest of the office to do it.

I feel thankful that this firm hired me many years ago. One of the reasons I've stayed with them is that the culture of the larger company reflects these processes we've put into place. There's no competition between advisors. We want each other to succeed.

Paul Fahrenwald didn't have to spend so much time helping me when I started. He didn't get any compensation for his time, yet he worked with me for weeks to help train me. Because of his assistance and the love of others who mentored me, I now coach new advisors on my own time. I appreciate people who poured into me, and I hope to pay them back by paying it forward.

Now, I'm grateful to have people in the office so I can go on vacation and everything seamlessly continues. Some of my clients worry about what will happen if I retire. Well, first, I love what I do, so I'm not planning on going anywhere for a long time. But second, our clear processes and the Eight Principles allow my team to act on my behalf and keep the business going. No one even notices when I'm out for a week.

How to Ask for Referrals

I don't want to leave you thinking no one in our office ever asks for referrals or introductions. We do. We include our request anytime it feels appropriate. It should feel natural, not forced.

First, we implement the Eight Principles so we deserve their referral. Asking for a referral without doing anything to warrant it will backfire. But after we're sure we brought our best to the table, we ask.

Our requests are always unscripted, but at the end of a meeting, you will sometimes hear us say something like this: "Thanks so much for allowing us to help you today. We appreciate you being with us for so many years. If I could replicate you one hundred times, I'd be the happiest financial advisor in the world. If you ever come across someone who needs help or asks questions about making investment decisions, I would be happy to talk with them. It could be some of your family or one of your friends, maybe even someone you work with. You've known us long enough to know we won't put a hard sell on them. So, if they just want to talk or get a second opinion, we would love to talk with them. I know if you introduce us to someone, they will be great people because you're so wonderful to work with."

Our goal when we ask is to avoid sounding salesy. Leaving out the word referral and offering genuine help to the people they care about puts them at ease. Many of them will talk about us anyway. We've built a friendship, and friends naturally refer friends; however, inviting them to make an introduction removes some of the questions. They might not realize we're looking for or taking new clients, and by truthfully complimenting them, they understand we really want to work with people like them.

A Gift to Yourself

While it was never our intention, this framework has become a tremendous gift to our office. We've proved the old adage 'opposites attract' false. In fact, science supports the idea of similarity attraction. Humans like to hang out and do business with people who share their values, interests, and ideals.[2] In our case, this translates to a mass of the most tremendous clients on the planet.

The people we work with each day are kind and generous. They show appreciation and respect. When we make a mistake, their graciousness is extraordinary. And as a bonus, the people they refer share those traits.

We love our clients. Not only because they trust us to help them, but also because they are tremendously nice people. When we make that first thank-you call after a referral, it usually includes something like this: "We truly appreciate the referral, and we can't wait to get to know them. We know, if they decide to work with us, they will be phenomenal clients because they are your friends."

The processes you build that incorporate these Eight Principles will quickly become the greatest gift you give yourself. They shouldn't be hard to follow. We keep them simple on purpose because we want them to be repeatable every single day.

Implementation

Johann Wolfgang Goethe once said, "At the moment of commitment, the entire universe conspires to assist you."

Being referable means committing to implementing processes that will make these principles a priority in your business and your life.

Each of The Eight Principles of the Referable Framework feels less than earth-shattering on its own. You already know how to do each one. Your company might already be practicing a few relatively well. However, exponential impact comes when you combine them. Even though I've shared them as eight individual principles, I'm sure you already noticed the way they intertwine. And when you learn to weave them into every part of your practice, they'll give you a business that gets people talking. The way these processes touch lives makes them transformational.

Take a minute and list the eight principles, leaving space to write between them:

1. Manners Invite You to Tables You Would Never See Otherwise
2. Talking Less Influences More
3. Your Interest in Others Makes You More Interesting
4. Clear Commitments and Follow Through Close the Trust Gap
5. Find Unique Ways to Reach Out to Let People Know You Care
6. Shortcuts Undermine the Long Game
7. Take Care of Your Team, and They Will Take Care of You
8. Communicate Compliments; Keep Complaints

Then answer these questions:

- What things are you already doing in each area to be referable? How can you tweak these to make them even better?
- In which areas are you missing the mark? What one thing can you implement right now to improve? What things would you like to add in three months, six months, nine months, and a year?
- What processes do you need to adapt or incorporate to ensure your company follows the Eight Principles?
- How often will you review your processes to ensure you're keeping yourself referable?

Thank You

Before I leave you, I want to thank you for taking time to read. If you made it this far, I'm guessing you are close to Natural Referability. You probably already practice many of the Eight Principles and have a loyal customer base. A bit of intentionality will easily bring your name to your client's holiday dinner table.

I appreciate you listening to my stories and thoughts, and I hope your day has become just a bit better for it.

Goethe finished his quote by saying, "Whatever you do or dream you can, begin it. Boldness has genius, power, and magic in it. Begin it now."

Endnotes

1   *The Inspired Home Show.* "Trust and Quality Most Important to Consumers' Perception of Value." March 6, 2023. https://www.theinspiredhomeshow.com/blog/trust-and-quality-most-important-to-consumers-perception-of-value/.

2   Stollznow, Karen Ph.D. *Psychology Today.* "Do Opposites Really Attract?" January 19, 2024. https://www.psychologytoday.com/us/blog/speaking-in-tongues/202401/do-opposites-attract.

Acknowledgments

TO MY FAMILY—JULIE, Sarah, Ben, and Rachel. Thank you for your love, your support, and your patience. You've been with me through all of it, and you remind me what truly matters. I love you so.

To our clients. Thank you for your trust, your loyalty, and the relationships we've built over the years. It is a privilege to walk alongside you and your families. Everything in this book exists because of what we've learned from you.

To my team. It's an honor to work alongside people who care so deeply about doing the right thing for others. A special thank you to Kendra and Karen for their partnership and leadership over the past eight years—you've been instrumental in building what we have today. And to Karen and Matt, thank you for the great start and the energy you bring to our team.

To Mom and Dad. Thank you for setting the example for Erin, Leah, and me. The lessons you taught—and continue to teach—have shaped who I am and will stay with me forever. And thank you for not only introducing me to Mister Rogers at such a young age, but for letting me watch it every day.

To my sisters and their families—the Reynolds and Doctor families—and to Julie's side of the family—the Petersens, Shannons, and Elsassers. Thank you for your love, support, and encouragement along the way.

To my grandparents, aunts, and uncles. Thank you for the values you passed down and the example you set. Grandma, those early conversations about investing shaped the course of my life more than you probably ever knew. The impact of those moments continues to live on in the work I do today.

To the friends who have supported and encouraged me throughout the years—especially the Jersey Boys and your parents, the Swenarton family, and my Villanova crew. I'm grateful for the laughter, the memories, and the influence you've brought into my life.

To the mentors and coaches who have shaped my thinking—Lee Brower and Dan Sullivan at Strategic Coach, Tom Bartow, Jason Selk, Don Connelly, Nick Murray, CEG Worldwide, and Ari Galper. Your guidance challenged me to think differently, grow intentionally, and build something meaningful. I'm deeply grateful for your influence.

To the many friends I've made along the way at my company, and to all of the people in the home office who work behind the scenes to support us. Your contributions make a difference every day, and I'm grateful for all that you do.

And finally, to everyone at Igniting Souls. Thank you for your help and guidance in bringing this book to life.

And to anyone striving to build a business rooted in relationships—thank you for being part of this journey. My hope is that these ideas help you create something that not only succeeds, but truly matters.

About the Author

DAVE VAN BUSKIRK is an author and Financial Advisor. With over 25 years of financial experience, he was named Principal in 2013. He earned a bachelor's degree in business administration from Villanova University and his MBA from Elon University.

He served as a regional leader for ten years, helping dozens of financial advisors grow their practices in the Dallas-Fort Worth area, where he was named a general partner in the firm.

Dave has been recognized as a Forbes SHOOK Best-In-State Advisor for the past several years, and his team has been consistently recognized for client service excellence within their firm.

With the support of his dedicated team, he enjoys being able to provide the highest level of service possible to his clients by meeting their needs and helping them achieve the financial goals that are most important to them. Dave and his wife, Julie, along with their three children, are very involved in giving back to their community.

CONNECT WITH DAVE

FOLLOW HIM ON
LINKEDIN TODAY.
@DAVEVANBUSKIRK

What If You Never Had To Ask For A Referral Again?
Learn How To Create A Business People Can't Wait To Recommend
SEND US A MESSAGE TO INQUIRE ABOUT SPEAKING OPPORTUNITIES

The Key To Being Rich is Knowing What Counts

Meet a financial advisor who takes the time to discover what truly matters to you and can help you create a financial plan to help support the life you dream of.

START THE CONVERSATION TODAY